fourteen poems

Issue 9

First published in 2022 by Fourteen Publishing.
fourteenpoems.com

Edited by Ben Townley-Canning.

Design and typeset by Stromberg Design.
strombergdesign.co.uk

Proofreading and copy editing by Lara Kavanagh.
lk-copy.com

Printed by Print2Demand Ltd, Westoning, Bedfordshire, UK.

ISBN:
978-1-7391697-2-5

Hello and welcome to Issue 9 of *fourteen poems*!

Nine issues is mind-blowing to me! When we launched three years ago, I wasn't sure if anyone out there would be as excited about contemporary queer poetry as I am. Turns out, there are a lot of you that love to geek out about LGBTQ+ poems and celebrate new poets too. I'm so thrilled that we're all here together!

Of course, if you're new to *fourteen poems* – welcome! We want to shine a light on queer poets, while celebrating stories from our communities. Lots of people are intimidated by poetry, so by keeping our poems limited to just 14 we aim to make poetry accessible for everyone.

This issue, I hope we've got a nice combination of critically acclaimed writers and names that might be new to you. I can't tell you how nice it is to see you all connect with particular poets or poems online, so if one of these poems speaks to you directly, please do share on social media and tag us! And follow these poets too – sharing, following, and connecting with poets online can really help new people find them and get excited too.

As always, we don't choose the poems by theme but I'm always excited about the connections that appear when the poems sit together. Looking at this issue, perhaps there's a sense of many of our poets looking back; childhood and its hopes and traumas, unrequited love, the freedom felt during that perfect night out, the complexities of family relationships, and the lure of Hollywood masculinity are just a few of the ideas that our poets explore.

But there's also hope for the future too: Jinhao Xie's subversion of myths to celebrate and create new ideas of queerness, Jay Whittaker's creation of a world that's safer for our future queer siblings, and Zara Meadows building new love "on the shoulders of/buried riot tableaux" are a few examples of this.

Dive in and discover more! I hope you enjoy and do let me know your favourites. I love hearing from you!

Ben Townley-Canning
Editor

Instagram:@14poems
Twitter: @fourteenpoems

PS If you'd like to subscribe and get our books landing on your doormat three times a year, head over to fourteenpoems.com/shop and subscribe now! Use the code QUEERBOOKS and save 40% on everything!

contents:

Seán Hewitt is a poet, writer, and critic based in Dublin, Ireland where he teaches Modern British & Irish Literature at Trinity College. His debut collection, *Tongues of Fire* (Jonathan Cape, 2020), was shortlisted for the Sunday Times Young Writer of the Year Award in 2021, and won The Laurel Prize in 2021. His critically acclaimed memoir, *All Down Darkness Wide* (Jonathan Cape), was released in 2022 and shortlisted for Biography of the Year at the Irish Book Awards. He was awarded the Rooney Prize for Irish Literature in 2022.

Instagram/Twitter: @seanehewitt

Immram

I was twelve, and woke alone
to a beautiful music. I was standing
by silver waters, and there was a branch
blossoming, suspended in the dark
above a mirrored pool. The air smelled
of saffron and of myrrh. I was twelve,
and the world arrived and shamed me
with its simplicity, so I sank myself
to the breast in the water. It shivered.
It threw icy hoops around me. Yes.
I felt ungendered in its arms. Even my skin
sang in its cold dress. It was not a dream.
Over the pool, the pale flowers
of the branch shifted slowly from pink
to gold, shaking down a flurry
of petals. I was being married
with the water. No, no witnesses –
but all night I moved inside it –
the blossoms turning blue, then mauve,
then white. Yes. I heard a sweet
silver bell. I tasted lavender
and frankincense. The soul, I knew,
was all plural. I could have spent
a thousand lives changing myself,
dipping my body over and over
in those bracing, fluent desires –

Seán Hewitt

Holly Moberley is a queer poet and Creative Writing MA graduate orbiting Somerset, UK. Her debut manuscript *Kinder Parasites* was shortlisted for the 2022 New Poets Prize and her poetry has been published in *Butcher's Dog* and *The North.* In 2021, she became Bristol's LYRA Slam Champion. Holly identifies her work as feminist diary entries from your weird cousin and is currently co-writing a theatre show on resuscitation, pop culture, and the 'drowning girl motif'.

Instagram/Twitter: @bird_and_thebee

What to Do When Nicole Kidman Doesn't Love You:

a hair-dying montage, hotels with swimming pools, inflatable flamingos, valuing my REM cycle,
scientology, pawning heterosexual jewellery,

boldly declining to experience a crush, crushing, being crushed,
telling my crush about said crush in question, resisting the urge to walk into a lamppost
while awaiting her voice note. her voice like nothing i've ever noted before.

i heard   that the red lights of amsterdam were first lit in the district of her mouth.
i heard   she was limping home in the after hours of an old european city like some mystical wolf.

how 12th-century gothic, how unintentionally twilight.

crush; she makes me want to listen to mazzy star,
she makes me want to mope around the house in an unwashed dressing gown.

in this light, i am like if a lava lamp was a girl. i am the gooey colour of gay panic.
to get there you have to take a left at clara's gym shorts and exit onto serena's surfer girl shoulders.

the difference between me and regency era dramas is that i hide my ability to evangelise.
i have been known   to cry into a fortune-telling mirror.
i have been known   to call this self care.

when you're a queer woman, anything you do becomes provocative.
you could be reclaiming rhinestones into your wardrobe
and all of a sudden it's because your crush is busy speaking to someone else.

i keep asking but my metaphors won't swallow me whole.
they say "no amount of pop-culture references can save you now"

but i'm a femme tom cruise on bad filler benders
and she's so nicole-kidman-post-divorce, it hurts.

Holly Moberley

Lady Red Ego is a Chinese/Scottish lesbian poet who has previously been widely published in anthologies, including *Re.creation* (Stewed Books, 2022), *We Were Always Here* (Queer Words Project Scotland, 2019), *Stay Home Diary* (Bitter Melon, 2020), *Crossing Lines* (Broken Sleep, 2021), as well as by magazines *The Dark Horse, 404 Ink, Lesbian Pulp*, and *Zarf Poetry*. Their debut pamphlet, *The Red Ego* (Wild Pressed Books), was published in 2019, followed by their second pamphlet *Natural Sugars* (Broken Sleep, 2020). Lady Red Ego's debut collection, *Your Turn To Speak!*, is due to be published with Blue Diode Press in 2023.

Instagram/Twitter: @ladyredego

Chinese Beer (A Love Poem for Kitty Tsui)

I saw you across the room, through
crowded ages. All those pale-haired
decades. Your hair as black as gravity.
Your hair black, just like me. Between
us, white butches weaved history into
their masculinities; the levi's and jawlines,
pretty boys with their pretty majorities.
Blue eyes blown wide with allyship,
attentively hanging onto every lesson
on my body. *Please don't ask me to*
meet your family. My jade hanging
heavier, every day, between my breasts,
weighing down the paper of my wings
as pink-skinned things fluttered up to
the ceiling. Oil and water mixing.
My jade, every day, darkening from
cerulean into royal waters. A King
of my own nation – an Emperor, even.
Vibrant, like me. Shocking to the masses.
Just like me, your mother could not hold
the word gay on her tongue. Same-d and
Sex-ed, the two of us. Diasporic dykehood
stretching us further, making us wait so very
much longer to see our own reflections, taste
our own liberations. You could pronounce
my name correctly; you, with the same pinyin
spelling of a sound that must be kissed out of
the mouth. Said with something stronger
than love. You with your tough-tender body,
built like a deity. That religion is native to me.
That sepia leather and skin. That Asian daring.
I saw you. I send this to you, a drink crossing
generations of loneliness, tall and cool and
thanking you.

Lady Red Ego

Sam Ross is an Irish American poet based in Brooklyn, USA. His book *Company* (Four Way Books, 2019) was selected by Carl Phillips for the Four Way Books Levis Prize in Poetry and received the 2020 Thom Gunn Award for Gay Poetry. He was an inaugural 2022 LGBTQ+ Artist in Residence at the Fine Arts Work Center in Provincetown.

Twitter: @samrawss

Fathoms

Resurrection never sounded like this
before this. It's spring.

The club's walls are wet, cyanotic
(it means drowned-colored, I think).

I'm washed in it.
The last time

I saw a shade like that
it was on the lips of a man

brawling surf, overwhelmed
by a swell that dragged him under, under,

away from shore. But we're not drowning.
It's spring. We're dancing. I pull you

through the floor.

Sam Ross

Spencer Wood is a poet and teacher based in Leeds, UK. His poems have been published in *Untitled Voices* and *Modern Queer Poets* (Pilot Press, 2019). Spencer recently read at the Leeds Poetry Festival and he runs the monthly LGBTQ+ Drama Club for Leeds Community Consortium.

Instagram/Twitter: @spenceriwood

Stanislavski's Dog

It's said an actor used to bring her dog to rehearsal   where it would nestle into a corner
and remain uninterested   by the human world of performance   but as the day's
work drew to a close   the dog would be at the door   lead in its mouth
Stanislavski believed the dog knew it was time to leave   as the actors began talking
naturally once more   from this came his challenge   to his cast to all actors
forever   get the dog to stand by the door

No matter how many ways I say   *mate*   it doesn't lift an eye but my brother says
faggot by accident   and it's scratching up the woodwork   howling to escape

Spencer Wood

Rupinder Kaur is a multidisciplinary artist based in Birmingham, UK. Her debut poetry book *Rooh* (2018) was published with Verve Poetry Press and she is currently further developing her one-woman show *Imperfect, Perfect Woman*, which debuted at Wolverhampton Literature Festival. She has also been a BBC New Creative and developed the audio piece *The Girls that Hide and Seek* (2021). She is currently part of Kali Theatre Discovery program (2021–2022), India-UK Creative Industries at 75, and Tara Theatre, Artists Make Space.

Instagram/Twitter: @rupinderkw

Trace

There's this photo where Mum's lips shine, cranberry wine.
No dark eyebags, she's with two girlfriends, all three stand
behind a foreign sun.

There's this painting Mum loves, Sohni In Heaven.
Meditating with her pitcher, did she become a Goddess? –
once away from the men.

There's this video Mum sent me, hands of young girls anchored
with bangles as they do the kikali barefoot in the dirt.
Their bangles going chan, chan, spinning so fast
they almost fall. Mum tells me one time a girl did.

There's this dream I had where I flicked seeds
on the garden shed roof until white doves spoke
to peach trees. One peach tree was Mum.
I am losing parts of Dad from my face.
I am becoming Mum, just taller,
so I can watch the doves fly for both of us.

Rupinder Kaur

Zara Meadows is a writer from Belfast, Northern Ireland. Their work can be found in *The Stinging Fly*, *Banshee*, *bath magg*, and *Honest Ulsterman*. They are currently studying at Queen's University, Belfast.

Instagram/Twitter: @zmameadows

Erin

Ireland is a place
& all at once it
isn't. Sometimes
I go there & wait
in the car for some-
thing to happen to
me, like a pile-up
of which I would form
the reliable base. I had no
form of reference as to
where you came from,
except Connswater. Who knew
Connswater could be so
beautiful. It lights itself
off loyalist bars & glistens
like a postcard scene:
Trevi Fountain at night, a
lunchtime Arc de Triomphe,
the incomplete Sagrada Familia
& all its golden scaffolding.
The Starbucks drive thru
rests on the shoulders of
buried riot tableaux. If we turn
out here, onto this road, is this
where my granny grew up?
Where yours did? I wonder
who brought who the milk
& bread when shit hit the fan.

Zara Meadows

AE Hines is a queer poet based in North Carolina, USA, and Medellín, Colombia. His debut collection, *Any Dumb Animal* (Main Street Rag) was released in 2021, and his work has recently appeared in *The Southern Review, Rhino, Ninth Letter, Greensboro Review, Poet Lore, Alaska Quarterly Review, Tar River Poetry*, and *I-70 Review.*

Instagram: @poet_aehines
Twitter: @poetaehines

Anxiety Disorder

I can't quite name this restlessness,
I tell him, not realizing this thought
has been spoken out loud.
But the restaurant is noisy,
our languages still strange to each other,
and he thinks I'm speaking
of the dressing on the salad
we're sharing, cannot place
the flavor.

Vinaigrette, he says,
popping his fork into his mouth,
this quiet longing for change
building in me faster than change
can come, the way certain plants
unable to wait for fall, bolt, leave
a wake of premature seed.
Honey,
he says, passing his fork, feeding me
one sticky green leaf impaled there.
Honey too, he says, withdrawing
steel from my mouth.

AE Hines

Jinhao Xie, born in Chengdu, is a Barbican Young Poet and a member of the Southbank Centre New Poets Collective 2021–2022. They are interested in nature, the mundane, the interpersonal, and personhood. Most of their work is inspired by visual and conceptual art, and can be found in *POETRY, Poetry Review, Harana, bath magg, Gutter Magazine*, and anthologies, including *Slam! You're Gonna Wanna Hear This* edited by Nikita Gill, *Instagram Poems for Every Day* by the National Poetry Library, *Re.Creation* (Stewed Books, 2022), and *Articulation to Keep the Light In* (Flipped Eye, 2022). Their love language is an act of service in forms of cooking for the beloved and quality time with meaningful conversations.

Instagram: @xie.jin.hao
Twitter: @jinisnotfound

Gabriel in the Pose of Pregnant Virgin

After Chris Ofili

He came; I too
Was masturbating
In this chaotic room: nebulous murk

Here is boundless Gabriel
Come
& meet me all this way & take me

As I am; bend me metallically back
Curvature of pleasure
Desiring to be taken in this wild fury

Aren't we FANTASTIC!
Paired wings; silica &
Molten limbs; pulsating lava

The sculptor forged me fruitless
Between my ribs; between my pelvic
Palace; Oh — G

-abriel! My pregnant angel
Messenger of my queerness

Touch these plumed breasts
Touch all this forgiveness
I exist to exist; to insist

My hollowed womb is intentional

Oh, Gabriel; we are impossibly
Beautiful; & I let you be
-ar my child; a sublime

Myth

Jinhao Xie

Alice Frecknall is a poet, short fiction writer, and fine artist. Her debut poetry collection, *Somewhere Something is Burning*, is published by Out-Spoken Press (2021). Her writing has appeared in a number of anthologies, including *bath magg*, *Butcher's Dog*, *The Stinging Fly*, and *Lightship Anthology*, and was shortlisted for the Out-Spoken Prize for Poetry 2022 and 2019, and the Lightship International Short Story Prize.

Instagram/Twitter: @alice_frecknall

Couples Therapy

We go two rounds, stop short,
God forbid either of us
should lose a tooth, heart; head
homewards through the fields,
pause to stick our fingers in
the mouth of an unsuspecting
goat chewing over a blade of
grass as if its friends aren't
already lying sized-up for
cutlets in the butcher's fridge.
The meat will be fall-off-the-bone
tender, just think! Crack and
grind of something small, cold
pain, threat of a blackout.

Alice Frecknall

Dior J. Stephens is a Midwestern, USA pisces and poet. He is the author of the chapbooks *SCREAMS & lavender*, *001*, and *CANNON!*. Their debut full-length collection, *CRUEL/CRUEL*, will be released by Nightboat Books in March 2023. Dior holds an MFA in Creative Writing from California College of the Arts and is currently pursuing a doctorate degree in Philosophy at the University of Cincinnati. Dior hopes to be a dolphin in his next life. Dior's preferred pronouns are he/they.

Instagram: @dolphinphotos
Twitter: @dolphinneptune

the [absence] of you

when i knew i'd lost you i flew

]to the other bloody coast
]memory in dancehalls
]backrooms
]candlelight
]most often in the morning

when i knew
]a part of me knew
]myself fresh,
]but what is there
        [to say]to]
[a body
[
[
]not
]to be found

]disposable sometimes
]most
]time,
]
]this sensation
]is
        ]man[
        i dont have memories of my father ever
telling me that he loved me

]sure
[at least a
]
]
].]
]surely,

]a whole lot else [
]the absence
]loud-silent disappointment
]black women [scorned
]music mother;
]now understood
]all this time
]the end of our cromwell
]where i waited]where i waited
]where i waited where
]i
]
]
]
]waited where i
]waited where i—

body feeling
]
]cinderblock
]to
]bend;

i'm glad i've stopped trying to make sense, or,
am making my own sense now.

Dior J. Stephens

Adriano Noble is a recent graduate of Durham University, and is currently based near Birmingham, UK. His work has been featured in *The Hellebore*, *Hungry Ghost Magazine*, and *Ink, Sweat and Tears*, as well as shortlisted for the Creative Future Writers' Award. He has work upcoming in *Rust & Moth*.

Twitter: @no_ao_

once again: romanticising cowboys

finally caved. got a suede fringe jacket off ebay. i've been pining for bonfires and songs that boom out of the sky, send birds of prey blooming out of sight and rock the cruel sun into an early tomb. onto saluting the sad cold nights! sweeter than the warm, demanding of whiskey & hoping you shiver. then i can slip the jacket from my form to yours (tho it don't look as good on you, forgive me), the fringe will sway seductively with the shift. i'll tell you once i burnt the bottom of a firepit out with vodka, almost lost my face when it roared swift as a stallion. & you might laugh or you might doubt my intellectual prowess. no matter. who has need for wiser lovers. shut me up with a cigarette, lit with our faces close and low. in this life i have a handlebar moustache, cover for a girlhood i fucked off (shit, maybe you got one too). nose-to-nose our moustaches almost don't touch whilst we dance slower and slower, slow as the foolish earth spins. annie proulx would be so mad that i read close range, looked at all that looming ache and thought i want a suede fringe jacket.

Adriano Noble

Christopher Lloyd is a writer and academic living in Bedford. He teaches contemporary literature and culture, and has published poems, stories, and essays in *Queerlings*, *Fruit Journal*, *Roi Fainéant*, *The Cardiff Review*, *Homology*, and elsewhere.

Instagram: @chrislllloyd9

Twitter: @clloyd9

after therapy I go on walks

at the end of my road is a community herb garden which is
not as fancy as it sounds   men often fight there over
cans of strongbow   muddle the rosemary with ring-pulls
& fag ends   tonight after self-scrutiny & warm
rain bats flicker in circles above me   the rose
sky embarrassed at its suppleness   I mark my year by
the bats' return   so much time has passed with such little
growth   of course the swallows come earlier & loop
so recklessly they must be showing off   there is
something piercing about the pipistrelles   they
remind me of my childhood lounge   the big windows
& open curtains   my dad didn't like to shut them
for reasons unknown to us   we watched as the bats
gestured in & out of view around the big oak   sail past
our row of houses as if marking territory   now I breathe
in wet mint & chives & watch them play above my head
like they're telling me something in another frequency

Christopher Lloyd

Jay Whittaker is a queer poet who lives and works in Edinburgh, Scotland. Her poems have been widely published in many journals, including *Poetry Review, The North, Butcher's Dog,* and *The Rialto*, and in the anthology *Staying Human* (Bloodaxe, 2022). She has published two poetry collections: *Sweet Anaesthetist* (Cinnamon Press, 2020) and *Wristwatch* (Cinnamon Press, 2018), which won the Scottish Poetry Book of the Year in 2018 in the Saltire Society Literary Awards.

Instagram/Twitter: @jaywhittapoet

Why flaunt it?

If we
don't leave a trace
how does anyone know
where to find us? Or who we were?
If we

aren't told
of folk like us,
ancestors, their lovers,
who, before us, trod the same path,
I mean

queer, yes,
in my sense and
theirs, visibly out there,
living and loving unashamed.
Yes, queer.

I mean
it's difficult
to realise. How can
anyone know who they are not,
knowing

nothing
of who they might
grow into, who they are?
Assumption is, we find our way
but we

stumble
longer, lonely,
lost. Imagine being
able to dream yourself, your selves;
follow

forebears
who made their mark:
queer, yes, unapologetic.
I'm writing this so when I'm dead
I leave

something,
a scratch on walls,
spare someone some effort
by knowing I, too, trod this path.
Queer, yes.

Jay Whittaker